To Talia Rachel Ross
Talia Rivka, bat Zvi Eliyahu

June 22nd, 2002

All our love on your Bat Mitzvah,
Aunty Susan, Uncle Malcolm, Daniel & David

Jerusalem,
The Enchanted Holy City

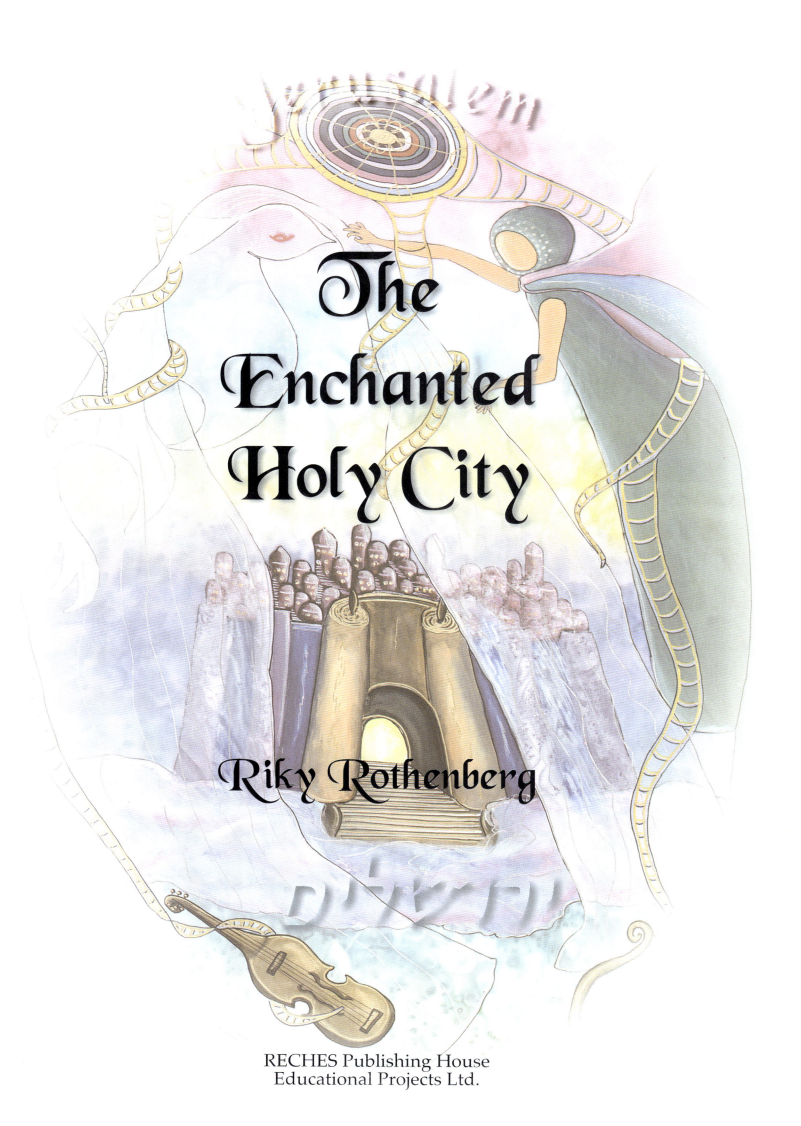

The Enchanted Holy City

Riky Rothenberg

RECHES Publishing House
Educational Projects Ltd.

רכס
הוצאה לאור
פרוייקטים חינוכיים בע״מ
ת״ד 75, אבן יהודה 40550

RECHES
Publishing House
Educational Projects Ltd.
P.O.B. 75, Even Yehuda 40550, Israel

עיצוב גרפי: ערן צירמן
עריכה לשונית עברית: שרה סורני
עריכה לשונית אנגלית: סטייסי ברוקס
צילום: סטודיו שוקי קוק, ישראל;
אוורט קואפרישין, ניו יורק

Graphic design: Eran Zirman
English editor: Stacey Brooks
Hebrew editor: Sara Soreni
Photographs: Studio Shuki Kook, Israel;
Everett Corp., New York

מסת״ב 0-114-403-965 ISBN
Printed in Israel

שַׁאֲלוּ שְׁלוֹם יְרוּשָׁלִָם יִשְׁלָיוּ אֹהֲבָיִךְ: יְהִי־שָׁלוֹם בְּחֵילֵךְ שַׁלְוָה בְּאַרְמְנוֹתָיִךְ:
לְמַעַן אַחַי וְרֵעָי אֲדַבְּרָה־נָּא שָׁלוֹם בָּךְ: לְמַעַן בֵּית־יְהוָה אֱלֹהֵינוּ אֲבַקְשָׁה
טוֹב לָךְ.

תהלים קכב:ו-ט

Pray for the peace of Jerusalem: they who love thee
shall prosper: peace be within thy walls, and prosperity
within thy palaces. For my brethren and companions'
sakes, I will now say, Peace be within thee. For the
sake of the house of the Lord our God I will seek thy
good.

Psalms 122:6-9

MEETING RIKY ROTHENBERG

D.E.: You will agree that it is quite rare to encounter an artist active within the rather evanescent boundaries of Jewish mystical art. What is the reason for such an uncommon choice?

R.R.: *During the last twenty-five years of my life I came as close as possible to mystical experience, to Jewish mystical experience. This kind of experience is holistic and influences all the sectors of one's life. It was not even a matter of choice. I felt compelled to give visual expression to the intense spiritual metamorphosis I was going through. I can say, in fact, that I underwent my mystical experience through the very act of painting.*

D.E.: I wonder how, in the context of a religious tradition where women have little access to study, a woman – moreover a woman artist – can make such a statement. It would seem that it is even harder when the the issue is the mystical way, which Scholem qualified as being "made for men by men." Do you come from a supportive background?

R.R.: *Yes and no. I had a solid and complete lay education. However, at the age of twenty I married a man who was professionally and personally interested in the apprehension of what he considered to be the backbone of the spiritual link between Man and Divinity in Jewish religious tradition, i.e., Kabbalah.*

D.E.: Is this when you started to paint scenes with kabbalistic subjects?

R.R.: *Not at all. At this time I was studying folk and colonial painting techniques in Peru. My first exposure to Jewish mysticism in general and to Kabbalah in particular did not extend beyond the spiritual domain. I was merely fascinated with this enchanted realm of symbols, conceptual models, practices, norms, and hope. I participated in any courses I could enroll in, I did some intensive reading, and little by little I started to teach. I never learned as much or progressed as quickly as when I had to prepare my own courses.*

D.E.: How soon did your direct involvement with Jewish mysticism find an echo in your art?

R.R.: *I cannot give an exact date because the process was gradual and slow. I believe that it took ten years before my spiritual journey found concrete expression in my artwork. At a certain moment I became aware that I had completely abandoned my previous themes and subjects: I was simply spellbound by the infinite world which was opening up before me.*

D.E.: How did the idea of the project, *Jerusalem, the Enchanted Holy City*, come to you?

I

R.R.: *It did not "come to me" – it grew in my mind and in my soul. It was my part of the Tree of Life, and I gradually became conscious of it. I realized, at a certain moment, that I was quite reluctant to part with my works having to do with Jerusalem, while I was selling practically everything else I was doing. Then I started to deliberately select my subjects in connection with the city and in the light of Jewish mysticism. When the Reches publishing house approached me with the proposal of doing a book on Jerusalem using my artwork, I had more than half of the fifty paintings ready. The fact that the project included, beyond the production of the book, international exhibitions of my work and the commission of a series of prints connected with each one of the paintings motivated me enormously.*

D.E.: Ambitious projects, which demand years of execution, leave behind not only the feeling of professional achievement and spiritual enrichment, but also of emotional exhaustion. Aren't you afraid of falling into a "niche" which commands repetition and imposes artistic routine?

R.R.: *The mystical domain is so vast that, no matter where you are, you have the feeling that you are just at the gate. I doubt that life is long enough to go much beyond the entrance. There are, however, so many enchanting mystical stations in its "path" (you know Hiroshige's* Tokaido Way?*) that I barely have patience to finish this project and return to my journey.*

(Interview by Dan Eban)

THE SILK ROAD TO THE ENCHANTED HOLY CITY

Visual artists, across all cultures and throughout all ages, share a loudly-expressed or carefully-hidden common dream. They yearn to dive head-first into a large-scale artistic project. There can be few incentives greater than this for spurring the artist's imagination, for prodding his "will-to-form,"[1] for straining his command of means and medium, in a word, for forcing him to give his very best – and more. For Riky Rothenberg, this dream came true when she was given the opportunity to complete, publish, and exhibit her vision of Jerusalem. The fifty original paintings in this book are milestones in an enthralling visionary quest begun ten years ago. Individually and all together, these works on silk are the result of an unremitting effort, the precious components of which were initiation and intuition.

Rothenberg's ultimate aim, she claims, was the visual embodiment of the unique mystical spirituality of Jerusalem.[2] This, as an advised reader will instantly concur, is easier to say than to do, and more facile to affirm than to prove. How is it possible to immure eternal spiritual matter in perishable, physical form? How can elusive and esoteric knowledge – accessible only to the mystic, and then only through painstaking efforts and supreme concentration – be hauled in, exposed on, and revealed by an arrangement of shapes and colors upon a flat surface?

Whether the onlooker is particularly patient or singularly hasty, the sense he experiences while going through Rothenberg's rich sequence of images may very well be the same. The hallmark of the whole is an ecstatic atmosphere of glory and splendor, sorrow and hope, awe and joy. This attempt at mood communication is granted through the choice of relevant subject matter, the use of recurrent motifs, the observance of consistent artistic conventions and composition rules, and the allegiance to a flamboyant style. While apparently sequential, the images do not tell a story. Although each one of the images comprises a self-sufficient scene, the body of work bespeaks unity. At the level of the visible, coherent lines, stable forms, and lavish colors are the warrants of optical and topical unity.

---

1. On the importance of the artistic intention, the *Kunstwollen* ("will-to-form") concept, see Alois Riegl, Stilfragen (Berlin: 1893), p. VIIff.

2. The creation of Jerusalem is, according to the artist's cosmogonic system, concomitant with the creation of the world (pl. 2). There is a rapport of consubstantiation between the Foundation Stone (out of which the world was created) and Jerusalem.

Underneath this state of visible unity, however, lies another one. At a deeper level, the onlooker may perceive an invisible unity which is a function of ideology. Riky Rothenberg's ideology is faith. I suggest that this formless, invisible ideology has a formative function and plays a determinative role in the choice of motifs, in their correlation, and mostly, in the creation of the image. Concomitantly, it is the state of organized faith which rules the endowment of the images with their mystical content.

Most of Rothenberg's scenery is located outdoors, but the landscape is an imaginary one. It is sometimes reminiscent of outdoors scenes in Persian miniatures, and often recalls Orientalist features fashionable in Eretz Israel painting from the beginning of the century. The extensive interplay between light and space confers upon the image a warm and radiant quality. This combination is so smooth and the flow so subtle that the two components seem to shift continuously into one another. What holds them together are the "paths" protracting into the light-space compound. At times, these "paths"[3] are only barely suggested through topographic features (pl. 23); at others, they are figured loosely by arboreal arrangements (pl. 43) or indicated by frail and wispy material contraptions such as the staircase of Jacob's dream (pl. 9). In most cases, these paths, lanes, avenues, or channels are softly defined by floating ladder-like appendages (pl. 10), ribbons of colored cloth, or strips of white fabric.

I believe that these allusive avenues leading to another reality are, allegorically, the ways of the *Pardes*. The concept of *Pardes* ('orchard' in Hebrew) and its use in Jewish religious exegesis are attributed to the great Spanish kabbalist Moses de Leon. In 1290 de Leon wrote a book entitled *Pardes*. Over the centuries the book was lost, but its message survived. *Pardes*, according to the author, is the grove of knowledge and understanding, an ideal site as near as possible to the Garden of Eden, i.e., Paradise. The Hebrew word *pardes* [פרדס] consists of four letters, each indicating a progressive level of understanding of Eternal Truth as spelled out in the Torah. The first level is that of literal meaning (*pshat*) [פשט], the second, of allegorical meaning (*remez*) [רמז], and the third, of scholarly interpretation (*drash*) [דרש]; the mystical secret revelation (*sod*) [סוד] constitutes both the final, fourth level and the supreme reward of the seeker.

Rothenberg relates to these superposed levels of knowledge in a simultaneous, and mostly subconscious, manner. Like the mystic, she undergoes an experience in which natural forms and natural laws are displaced and metamorphosed. And like the mystic, the artist tries

---

3. "The Sefer Yetsirah (The Book of Creation) opens with the statement: 'By means of thirty-two mysterious paths did the eternal, the Lord of Hosts, engrave and establish His name and create His world. The 'thirty-two paths' are the twenty-two letters of the Hebrew alphabet and the ten 'Sefiroth'." Sidney Spencer, Mysticism in World Religion (Harmondsworth, England: Penguin Books Ltd., 1963), p. 180.

continuously to communicate – as paradoxical as this may sound.[4] *Pardes* is, by definition, an extraordinary system of communication. It imposes sense and order upon human experience. The system's elements have at once polymorphic and ultimate meanings; its channels are simultaneously hierarchically differentiated, linked, and interchangeable. Its whole posits a unified force field of the possible encounter between human and divine. *Pardes*, then, is the invisible ideological foundation upon which the visible unity of Rothenberg's imagery relies.

In order to render public the images of an inner journey, the artist – again, like the mystic – must rely upon symbols. These symbols are multiple and diverse: religious and mystical, personal and ethnic, ancient and modern, transparent and esoteric, historical and eternal. As one might expect, any given symbol carries more features than the dominant quality defining it. I will divide the artist's symbols, for the moment, into two classes: hard symbols and soft symbols. The difference between them is based not on texture, but on the strength of their formal definition. When the form is constant, easy to recognize, and used in a prominent location, I refer to it as a hard symbol. Jerusalem and the image of the Godhead, to name a few, are hard symbols (pl. 10). When the symbol is suggested more than revealed, when its depiction is polymorphic more than uniform, when it relies upon arrangements and interactions rather than objects and entities, or when its expression depends upon elements of color and rhythm rather than of form and line, then I call it a soft symbol. I recognize among the soft symbols the glorious polyphony reigning in many of the works (pls. 4, 22), the attitude of rapture of the would-be human images, the radiant expanse of mellow, yellow light of transcendental origin (pl. 40), and particularly the weightless gliding of figures and objects along the thread of an invisible ascendant spiral.[5] In spite of the apparent dichotomy, the conceptual fabric of hard and soft symbols is, as I will show, both interrelated and complementary.

The Godhead is a dominant and complex symbol.[6] In most of the scenes it is composed of an abstract symbolic element and a formal sign. In many scenes the Godhead symbol appears in

---

4. Gershom Scholem, <u>Kabbalah and Its Symbolism</u> (New York: Schocken Books, 1969), p. 8.

5. This virtual spiral (i.e., implied but not formally represented) receives, in one case, a concrete visual form (pl. 38).

6. The terms symbol, sign, and icon designate visual elements signifying well-defined concepts. Their meaning is differently interpreted by various authors, and the terms are sometimes understood differently in common and academic language. When there is no formal connection whatsoever between the concept and the signifier, then the visual element is a symbol – such as the lily for purity. When there is a partial linkage, as in the case of a pair of padded gloves standing for boxing, we speak of a sign. In common language, the term "icon" has generally designated a certain type of Orthodox Christian painting portraying Christ, the Virgin Mary, or saints and martyrs. Today, and from the functional point of view, an icon is understood to be a visual element that conveys important cultural

conjunction with another visual element – an icon. In some cases, this icon is a third component of the Godhead symbol. The symbolic element is a nearly-circular image formed by concentric colored layers and lines. In the physical world, the image evokes the cross-section of a petrified tree. Sometimes the image contains tiny lines directed inward towards the center of the image or pointed outward like the rays of the sun or the cilia of some primordial living cell. In certain works, multiple circular images are mobilized for iconographic reasons or compositional requirements (pl. 12). In all cases, two or more semi-transparent, tapered, ladder-like appendages are attached to the periphery of the circular element. These appendages generally unfold in a wide curve across the scenes. Undulating and serpentine, they contribute to the division of the image into a central, focal, medallion-like zone and a peripheral, supportive background. Often the medallion, the sacred precinct, is completed by the subtle and sensuous sway of a white cloth shawl, tenderly held by one or more white doves (pl. 14). In *Light for All* (pl. 19), this wide band of white cloth is attached to the circular element and reinforces the sinuous movement of the ladder-like appendages.

In a *Pardes* frame of reference, the nearly-circular symbolic element signifies the concept of the *Sefiroth*[7] or divine emanations, at once qualities and agencies of God. Through this expanse of divine energy, a transcendent God becomes immanent in the world. The ladder-like appendage

---

affects or numinous qualities. From the structural point of view, the icon is an isomorph, that is, an image-to-scale of an object which is highly suggestive of a certain concept. The crown, for example, is a worldwide icon for royalty. See Dan Eban, "Does Art Really Communicate? And If So, How?," Art As a Means of Communication in Pre-Literate Societies (Jerusalem: The Israel Museum, 1990), p. 411ff.

7.   The concept of the *Sefiroth* is at the center of a vast symbolic system. Within this system, the names of the *Sefiroth* are more than sheer abstract qualifiers. Kabbalists have seen them as keys which designate and deliver various kinds of divine energy. They are divided into three triads, with a tenth representing the harmony of them all. The first triad is composed of *Keter* (Crown), which is indistinguishable from *En-Sof* (the Infinite) and from the mystical 'Nothing', *Hokhmah* (divine Wisdom), and *Binah* (divine Intelligence). In the second triad there are *Hesed* (divine Love or Mercy), *Din* (the Power or Justice of God), and *Tifereth* (divine Beauty). The third triad consists of *Netsah* (Victory), *Hod* (Glory), and *Yesod* (Foundation). The tenth, known as *Malkhuth,* which is the divine Kingdom or *Shekhinah,* signifies the presence of God in the universe, including His special manifestation in the lives of men. See Spencer, Mysticism in World Religion, p. 191ff.
     According to another kabbalistic interpretation, the ten *Sefiroth* form a tree which was originally planted by God and which became the image of God; by way of this tree, God's energies flow into the process of Creation. This circular image (which has neither beginning nor end) throws a complementary light onto a symbolic fabric in which the conceptual shifts into the organic, and abstract principles metamorphose into the life force. See Scholem, On the Kabbalah and Its Symbolism, p. 94.

is a sign of ascension. Literally, it may relate to Jacob's ladder. Metaphorically, the sign seems to indicate the existence of a way for the faithful. Finally, at the level of talmudic interpretation, the sign marks the inherent capacity of man to reach a complete union with God.

The strip of white cloth, directly or indirectly connected to the Godhead, is in itself a powerful Jewish icon. It is obviously related – especially when decorated with black transversal lines at its fringed end – to the prayer shawl (*talith*). At the literal level, it betokens the act of praying. At the allegorical level, it denotes the mandatory practices (*mitzvoth*) the Jew must observe in order to define himself. On a higher interpretative level, the icon marks the Jew's role as God's partner in the task of perfecting the order of the living world (*tikkun*). The wide open, arm-like expanse of the ladder-like appendages and *talith* allude to divine control, guidance, and protection for the people of Israel. Ultimately, the Godhead symbol with its ladder-like appendages is evocative of divine commitment to the destiny of the People of Israel. The *talith*, conversely, bespeaks the Jew's commitment to fulfill God's commandments.

The ascendant movement is a generic soft symbol in the artist's work. While it is true that we cannot detach the force of the movement from the 'human figures' and inanimate objects being moved (without the floating forms, the symbol could not exist), it is clear that the particulars of the symbol are the very act of floating, the ascension itself, and its spiral trajectory and target. The 'human figures' and 'flying objects' (especially musical instruments) are but the material indicators of this exceptional state of weightlessness and levitation. The soft symbol of the ascendant movement echoes the complexity of the symbolic construct of the Godhead even if it is, perforce, less structured. Levitation as a symbol of man coming closer to the divine has a long history. By the emphatic cancellation of the law of gravity, the artist deliberately transgresses the border between natural and supernatural. The artistic discourse is transferred from the realm of physical reality into a magical, religious, or mystical domain. Hellenistic art disseminated the motif of the floating figure – love god or wind god – which is probably the ancestor of the Christian angel. However, with the exception of some Annunciations, there is little ecstasy in the appearance of the flying angels. Their mighty feathered wings seem, paradoxically, to confute spirituality.

Rothenberg's interpretation of the upward movement is a notable departure from Christian scenes of the Ascension. These are scenes in majesty. Their protagonists (the Savior or His Mother) are not doing anything: they are just there, hovering in splendor and glory. If they appear to be in motion, it is because they are picked up from above or pushed up from within. Conversely, Rothenberg's figures are expressly active and directly engaged. An energetic ascendant movement is suggested by their posture and location, arm movements, head inclination, and dress shape with its banner-like flaps swaying in the ether. In an indefinite, lavish, polychromic space, the weightless figures seems to ride the draft at will (pl. 29) with no need for feathered contraptions.

The meaning of the ascendant movement is wide and complex and directly determined by the identity of the figures. These 'characters' can be divided into the large, often single figures featured in central positions and the smaller, accompanying ones in peripheral locations. The majority of the figures engaged in the act of ascension are wearing female dress and are featureless. (Are these 'human figures' portrayed as featureless in deference to *halakhic* laws interdicting depiction of the human face?) A close examination of the figures reveals the emptiness hidden under their capes and hoods, recalling the nothingness trapped in the armor of Italo Calvino's nonexistent knight.[8] In this open system of communication which is the Torah in its *Pardes* mode, the Nothing is nothing other than a divine attribute, a part of the *En-Sof* (the Infinite), which is one of God's qualities and names. In the "floating" context of Rothenberg's images, the nothingness is evocative not of material default but of spiritual energy.

The mass of void trapped under the fabric of the small, upward-gliding figures signifies for Rothenberg the *Neshamah*, that part of the human soul which is of divine origin.[9] The *Neshamah*, i.e., the soul proper – essentially different from the *Nefesh* (the life force) and the *Ruah* (the spirit) – soars upward to meet the divine, of which it is an intrinsic part. Its task is to carry with it the rest, or at least a part, of the human soul. The quantity is determined by the quality of man's involvement in the act of "correcting" himself and mending the world (*tikkun*).

The other floating figures, when they are conspicuous and prominently located, denote the *Shekhinah*.[10] The last of the divine emanations, the *Shekhinah* is also known as *Malkhuth* (Kingdom). Kabbalists have attributed to this emanation manifold cardinal tasks and qualities. They have described it as a the feminine principle in God, as God's daughter and bride, as the symbol of eternal womanhood, as the personification of the Congregation of Israel, and finally, as the mother of each individual Israelite. The *Zohar* recounts that "the Sefiroth as a whole, are . . . the offspring of the union between God and the Shekhinah . . ."[11] The only emanation detached from God and projected into the world, the *Shekhinah* strives to return from Exile (*Galuth*) and reunite with God.

---

8. The hero of Italo Calvino's novel Il Cavaliere Inesistènte is a medieval warrior who thinks, speaks, loves, and fights regardless of his being no more than a voice emerging from a dynamic but empty suit of armor. (Milan: Arnoldo Mondadori Editore, 1993).

9. The artist also uses the flame, a cross-cultural symbol for the soul, to designate the *Neshamah* (pl. 27).

10. In certain kabbalistic systems, the connection between the concepts of *Shekhinah* and *Neshamah* reaches the level of complete identity. Scholem, On the Kabbbalah and Its Symbolism, p. 106.

11. Spencer, Mysticism in World Religion, p. 192.

The conceptual affinity between the *Shekhinah* and the *Neshamah*, signifying related stages of the same process (i.e., the process of redemption), echoes the functional affinity between the Godhead and the *talith* which conditions the encounter between human and divine. The soft symbol of the ascendant movement reinforces and expands messages of guidance and divine protection embedded in and carried by the hard symbol of the Godhead.

The hard symbol of the Godhead and the soft symbol of the movement of ascension constitute the two poles of a structural axis perceptible both at the visible, painterly and at the invisible, conceptual, level. This axis is centered by or balanced through the presence of another element, the eponymic element of the entire body of work, namely, Jerusalem.

The image of **Jerusalem, the Enchanted Holy City,** is a cardinal icon in Rothenberg's body of work. Its function is that of a metaphysical turnpike, an expressway channeling numinous energy and transcendental exchange. The first known visual representation of Jerusalem appears in the mosaic map of the Byzantine church of Madaba in Jordan. It dates from the sixth

Map of Jerusalem, Byzantine mosaic
Madaba, Jordan, 6th century C.E.

century C.E., but the motif was probably older. There is striking formal and conceptual similarity between Rothenberg's interpretation and the Madaba image. Both are composed of dominant, tall, cylindrical buildings, brown in color and surrounded by walls. Their format is geometrical – oval for the Madaba motif and either oval or rectangular in most of the Rothenberg variants. Each of the icons imparts the feeling of a very dense, compact construct. Indeed, the two icons share a graphic quality analogous to the kind of stylized image embedded in a seal. This extensive formal resemblance is challenged, however, by a striking structural divergence. While the Madaba icon has a cognitive origin and historiographic purpose, the Enchanted Holy City icon is the fruit of an inner vision and proposes an ahistorical perspective. Its visual strength is rooted in its surroundings, namely the numinous atmosphere reigning in the artist's scenery. This numinous atmosphere then confers upon the whole scene an iconic quality. The motif of the Enchanted Holy City, therefore, has the value of an 'icon within an icon'. This kind of visual confrontation secures a rapid passage from the presumable concrete domain (the city) to the overt metaphysical realm (the setting) and vice versa, lending the scene a vibrant, dynamic quality.

A fleeting survey of the body of work may bring some insight into the way in which the artist activates the Jerusalem motif. Its size is generally constant, although it is sometimes adjusted to meet new composition and content requirements. Occasionally, the city acquires architectonic presence and expands conspicuously, in both surface and bulk, to become the dominant feature of the scene (pl. 35). The motif is represented in most but not all of the scenes. Often, the celestial Jerusalem and the terrestrial Jerusalem are depicted simultaneously. This ideological cohabitation leads to the creation of an impressive power field, the fabric of which is seldom visible, but the effects of which are striking (pl. 29). This power field abolishes the requirements of local and temporal definition and enforces the certitude of a mystical location. In certain cases the power field comes into being when the Jerusalem icon and the Godhead symbol enter into a synergetic relation (pl. 10).

Formally stable in most of the scenes, the Jerusalem motif sometimes acquires new shades of identity. In certain scenes, for example, a new form, such as that of a pitcher (pl. 20), an oil lamp (pl. 27), or even the mouth of a volcano (pl. 2) is attached to it or imposed upon the Holy City icon. The Jerusalem-Godhead compound (pls. 5, 47) is much more than a simple graphic addition. Forging new avenues for thought and feeling, it is undoubtedly the most powerful of all the merged motifs.

Significantly, the Jerusalem icon seems never to have any physical contact with the ground, even when it features the terrestrial Jerusalem. In most cases, the Enchanted Holy City is hovering in an undetermined space or floating upon a shiny cushion of air and light. In its flying variant, the icon is integrated within the slow ascendant spiral movement, emblematic of the encounter between human and divine.

The Jerusalem icon is sometimes reduced to the stature of a sign (see note 7). In these cases, a sole feature of the city, such as a gate, the wall, or even the Wailing Wall, is used to denote the whole. The "gate" sign, a typical *pars pro toto*, might be located in the wall (pl. 34), take the form of a porch (pl. 37), or be represented totally detached from the rest of the icon (pl. 33). It is often conceptually associated with the way of the Torah, linked visually to the symbol of Divine Light (pl. 4), and related empathically to the arrival of the Messiah. Like the Jerusalem icon, the gate sign has important formal and conceptual plasticity. Rothenberg employs a double depiction of the detached motif to denote the Tablets of the Law (pl. 15). In a glorious architectonic expanse, the sign signifies the Temple (pl. 36). This last image has obvious Christian (the conch shell) and Muslim (the *mihrab* arch) connotations. A genuine ideological manifesto, the image comes as close as possible to the the embodiment of the mystical passage to the Holy of Holies.

Over the years, thematic perseverance has endowed Rothenberg's visual language with such a degree of coherence and intensity that she has has succeeded in articulating a true system of communication. Although this system is built upon mainstream Jewish mystical tradition, the message that it organizes and channels is both modern and personal. The system's vocabulary consists of three registers, each composed of a limited number of motifs. Some are recurrent motifs, appearing in most of the scenes, while others are specific to one or a few of them. Simultaneously activated, the registers function like the various sound-producing sections of an organ. The melody is collective, but each voice maintains its individuality. The first such register is composed of prominent recurrent motifs. In order of frequency I mention the dove,[12] the *talith*, the veil (which is very much connected to the *talith*), the anthropomorphic figure (when it does not denote a biblical character), the Divine Light, the *Pardes* garden, the Tree of Life, and the three motifs we have already analyzed – Jerusalem, the Godhead, and the movement of ascension. The application of silver and gold lines that the artist uses to enhance certain significant details also has the value of a recurrent motif. Like the ascendant movement and Divine Light motifs, it has low figurative resolution but great symbolic value. The use of precious metals (especially gold) in mystical pictorial contexts has connotations ranging far beyond its mere visual, decorative purpose. It was employed profusely in Byzantine art – "the purest form of religious art"[13] – to form the background for holy images. A multi-evocative symbol in its own right, gold signifies divine light, glory, preciousness, incorruptibility, permanence, and transcendence.

The second register is built up of motifs that recur with moderate frequency and display a marked topical organization. A group of motifs pertaining to the same theme is activated within the scene to reinforce the artist's message. In this register I recognize the themes of musical instruments, vegetal motifs (especially those denoting the nourishing plants), animal imagery (which frequently channels a secondary message), and distinctive Jewish motifs such as the shofar, the Tablets of the Law, *tefillin* (phylacteries), the menorah, Torah scrolls, the Star of David, and the olive branch, symbolizing redemption. Finally, we should also mention here a group of igneous motifs comprising flames, torches, and candles. The light they cast is evocative of the soul *(neshamah)*, sacred knowledge, and the way of the Torah (pl. 26).

The third register consists of highly specific motifs which are used only once or twice. In most cases they are biblical characters (pl. 14), although they may also be biblical or Aggadic symbols, e.g., the Foundation Stone in *The Creation of the World* (pl. 2). On rare occasions they are even

---

12. This symbol appears for the first time in the synagogue of Maon, Byzantine period, 583 C.E. Raymond Cogniat, <u>Genie du Judaisme Tresors de l'Art Juif</u> (Paris: Bernard Levraut, 1975), p. 54.

13. Herbert Read, <u>The Meaning of Art</u> (England: Penguin Books, 1951), p. 85.

signifiers of modern concepts, such as the knot from *Declare My Glory among the Nations* (pl. 46), which symbolizes mankind.

A certain number of "rules" lend to this visual system its syntactic legitimacy. Implicitly, they have made it as intelligible as the nature of esoteric matter will permit. The pool of motifs is limited, but, as in a chess game, there is an endless number of possible combinations. Each different combination forms a fabric into which the artist has woven various mystical threads. Prominent recurrent motifs are particularly multi-evocative. The anthropomorphic figure, for example, may alternately – or simultaneously – signify the People of Israel, the *Shekhinah*, an archangel, or the *Neshamah*. The registers, which are a function of grouping and hierarchy, are not completely closed. A given motif may vary with regard to its status or structural location. Thus, the recurrent motif of the gliding dove holding a *talith* or veil in her beak and signifying the *Shekhinah* can become a specific symbol and harbinger of the modern peace message (pl. 40). As in other systems of communication, the impact of the message is reinforced by reiteration. The message is fortified through the agency of a number of different correlative motifs. In *The Hasmonean Wars*, war is signified by fire, elephants, and weaponry (pl. 26). Consequently, the signifiers become interchangeable. In *The Destruction of the Temple* (pl. 23), both the child accompanied by the *Shekhinah* and the gliding dove signify the same concept: the People of Israel heading for trouble, as symbolized by a thick layer of heavy clouds. The fact that in this day of sorrow and desolation the dove is drifting in front of the Divine Light portends optimistic expectations for an indefinite future time.

The conjunction of two disparate motifs can lead to the formation of a totally new message which does not preexist in each of the individual motifs. The true nature of time becomes apparent when one realizes that in *The Flood* (pl. 5), the ark and the Tower of Babel are depicted at the same referential level. The two motifs refer more to the beginnings of the People of Israel than to the precise events with which they are connected. In a work with obvious programmatic qualities, Jerusalem is coeval with the creation of the world (pl. 2). Given the mystical content of her quest, it makes sense that the time construct at work in Rothenberg's visual system is continuous and homogeneous rather than historical and sequential. In continuous time, natural temporal modules are replaced by divine, atemporal parameters. If all notions of real time have been abolished, it is no wonder that the moon and the sun are shining synchronously in the sky (pl. 2). It is not a miracle: it is the rule. This concept of continuous time is essential to the communication system's capacity to translate the mystical journey into visual terms.

The concept of space fulfills a similar function. The dominant spatial construct in the entire body of work is a flat or partially-flat unnatural model, built up from a set of colored surfaces and some shallow volumes (pl. 14). The edges of the picture's planes are ambiguous, and it is difficult to know where one ends and another begins (pl. 33). As in *The Creation of the World* (pl. 2), where motifs are simultaneously seen frontally (the floating Godhead), from above (the Primordial

Waters), and from below (the flying figures), multiple viewpoints are at work in all the paintings. A theater of extraordinary events, this spatial construct is inhabited by such disparate "items" as symbols, supernatural figures, everyday objects, landscape features, and architectonic constructions. If the time construct is continuous and homogeneous, the spatial construct is heterogeneous and composite. Unfit to denote the common apprehension of reality, this conceptual spatial construct is perfectly adapted to the projection of a mystical vision. Moreover, a mystical vision by its very nature requires an indefinite space.

If the space depiction is ambivalent, the organization of the pictorial frame and the definition of figurative motifs eschews equivocation. The frame is firmly secured by the combination of a strong center (pl. 28) with either a dominant vertical median (pl. 2) or an attention-grabbing medallion (pl. 14). The motifs are defined by hard edges and sinuous outlines, generally encasing densely colored surfaces. The surfaces are simple shapes, cut out like a tailor's templates and schematically assembled. Often, they are enhanced with minute details. The artist's interpretation of the pictorial plane reflects, consciously or not, the function she attributes to her message carriers. Having something to say and wanting to be heard, the artist opts for the directness of a graphic message. Figurative motifs and the pictorial plane carry the first message to the onlooker. Beyond all else, they have an ideologic and didactic purpose. Once the onlooker is engaged, hard definitions of any kind begin to melt, and through subtle manipulations of light and color, the viewer is lured into the arcanes of the mystical path.

The interplay among the artist's technique, support medium, and color application leads to the creation of an active textural compound which conveys a large share of Rothenberg's message. Clearly, the artist's most significant decision was her choice of the sensuous silk fabric. Rothenberg has succeeded in raising silk to the level of glass[14] as a justified vehicle of the mystical message. The challenging textile permits a subtle spreading of washes with a gradual passage from saturated zones to very dilute ones. At a later, second stage, it absorbs equally well the fine-line watercolor drawings and the deep chromatic zones of applied acrylics. Finally, it is receptive to the impression of silver and gold highlights which concludes the technical process.

The choice of silk as support medium permits not only fine tuning of the differently saturated chromatic zones (pl. 22) but also the creation of areas of heightened transparency (pl. 26). This kind of expanded porthole, through which the gaze penetrates into the meanders of the mystical projection, is the allegorical equivalent of an initiatory ritual. Transparency, alluding to a common source of spirit and substance, is a hallmark of Rothenberg's style.

---

14. Glass was and still is used as support medium for folk painting with mystical connotations in many East European countries.

Highly coherent throughout the entire body of work, the artist's style relies as much on color as it does on line. In this regard, there seems to be a certain functional division between the watery, airy hues of the background, inducing a metaphysical atmosphere, and the more precise, heavy chromatic areas directly connected with well-defined symbols. The extensive color symbolism, originating from Kabbalist lore and the artist's free associations, increases the impact of the messages encoded in the figurative and non-figurative motifs. *Light for All* (pl. 19) makes a convincing case. Here, the subject matter is neither the flame nor the fire, but the enlightenment one reaches through the Torah. The three candles (three being the number of the biblical fathers) indicate that the central figure signifies Man in the generic sense. His robe is red, red being a transcultural symbol of love. The message, therefore, is that Man, animated by love for God, activates the Torah through his study and observance; it is this synergistic act which brings light to mankind.

During her mystical journey, the artist handles an impressive number of concepts through the agency of a handful of visual motifs. I have tried to show that, at the conceptual level, the *Pardes* system imposes order and reason across the entire body of work. The striking stylistic unity throughout makes the projection of the mystical journey intelligible at the formal level. We have seen that various stylistic elements, such as movement, line, shape, volume, space, color, and composition, have complementary effects, permitting the apprehension of a totally supernatural scene at a certain level of reality. A case in point is the issue of size and proportion. To this end, three interesting facts should be mentioned. First, it appears that the artist made no attempt to submit all the motifs of a given image to a standard scale. For example, certain figures are higher than the hills on top of which they are standing (pl. 6). Secondly, even motifs of the same kind, such as figures, are not subject to the same size canon. Mast-like principal characters dwarf the secondary ones (pl. 30).[15] Finally, the figure's canon, especially that of the main figure, is of Byzantine or Gothic type, i.e., elongated (pl. 3).[16] A state of disproportion reigns. This state is monitored in the sense that the disproportionality is congruent from scene to scene. This approach is highly characteristic of artistic representations in artistic traditions where spirituality was the cardinal subject matter.

---

15. The enlargement of figures of outstanding importance is one of the essentials of Byzantine art. See David Talbot Rice, Byzantine Art (Harmondsworth, England: Penguin Books, Ltd., 1968), p. 50.

16. Tamara Talbot Rice, in her discussion of the style of Russian icons (an offshoot of Byzantine art) by the end of the fourteenth century, notes that "the figures now become strangely elongated, in the intensity of their desire to reach unto heaven. Sometimes they stand on tip-toe, as if to narrow the gap, and their gestures, though still restrained, definitely indicate emotion . . ." See Ikonen (London: Batchworth Press, 1962), p. 16.

Religious artistic traditions have been the object of extensive analysis. But can we differentiate between religious and mystical art? Religious art is an artistic tradition in which religious events are evoked and religious motifs utilized. Manner, motifs, and subject matter enjoy collective clerical and lay acceptance. Stylistically, it may stretch from an overtly naturalist mode to conceptual and abstract representation, while its mystical content may oscillate from high to nil.

Mystical art is a form of religious art. Manner, motifs, and subject matter are strongly determined by the artist's unique and personal religious experience. The style is always non-realistic and conceptual, and its mystical content is conspicuous and dominant. On the basis of Rothenberg's artistic statement, we may reach not a definition, but an intelligible description of the essentials of mystical art. Specifically, the artist's style is non-realistic and flamboyant. It leads to the construction in continuous time of a metaphysical and indefinite space. This space is inhabited by many flat forms with sinuous, hard-edged outlines and a few shallow volumes. The artist fancies both dazzling and deep colors, central compositions, motifs sized according to status, and careful, minute detail. She has created a train of monumental miniatures of religious subjects by utilizing old and new religious motifs, the new ones being her own personal inventions. Her characters originate both out of the world of common experience and from a transcendent, higher reality in which the laws of nature are nullified. A movement of ascension hinting at the encounter between human and divine forms the core of the artistic statement. Feelings of elation are expressed by posture and gesture and through music and dance in an atmosphere of ecstasy, bathed in a glorious celestial light. The invisible ideological threads of esoteric mysticism are woven into an indivisible net of content and style.

This cluster of features may be as close as we can come to the *identikit* picture of mystical art. Certain comments of Kathleen Raine about William Blake,[17] one of the greatest mystical artists of all times, reinforce this assumption. In connection with Blake's treatment of form, Raine says: "The linear style is, in fact, characteristic of religious art; and always Blake insists that the 'spirits', whether of men or gods, should be 'organized' within a 'determinated' and bounding form."[18] This form, Raine goes on to emphasize, is that of an "outline without volume . . ."[19]

---

17. William Blake (1757–1827), poet, printer, mystical painter, and art theoretician, was one of the most enthralling artistic figures of his time. His analysis of the aims and means of religious art has maintained its relevance till today. Kathleen Raine concludes that "It is his gift of communicating his vision . . . that entitles Blake to so high a place." See William Blake (London: Thames and Hudson, 1970), p. 8. One of his masterpieces was the mystical poem *Jerusalem. The Emanation of the Giant Albion*. It was accompanied by one hundred watercolors, in the execution of which Blake invested years of work. More than coincidence, one may assume a certain meeting of minds.

18. ibid., p. 20.

Not less relevant are Blake's cardinal concepts of time and space, and finally, his vision of life (here, I mean spiritual life): "Against the mechanistic view of nature, product of the rational mind . . ., Blake proclaimed life. Life is non-spatial and non-temporal; gravity does not weight it down, nor bulk contain it."[20]

This conceptual concordance between two artists separated by so vast a historical and cultural gap is significant. Moreover, it raises an important question. How is it possible that artists hailing from such different times and places similarly expressed what is supposed to be a very personal experience?

I would suggest that it could not possibly be otherwise. Riky Rothenberg did not, after all, invent the visual conventions of mystical art; rather, she recreated them. Not belonging to a mystical artistic tradition upon which she could rely, she forced precious spiritual ore into a tight and accurate set of visual forms. Virtually a self-taught artist, she found, at the deep end of her inspiration well, insights and emotions that were mainly her own. If her formal language shows intriguing similarities with that of other mystical artists, it is because a certain kind of human experience fosters a certain kind of artistic response. The transcultural stability of this response is a magnificent instance of the cardinal artistic rule: **form follows spirit.**

I would not want anyone to come away from this discussion with the impression that the mystical quest and the artwork itself are two separate entities. If I have divided them, it was only for analytical reasons. Riky Rothenberg's paintings are accompanied by related quotations from biblical, Aggadic, or talmudic texts. However, Rothenberg's paintings are neither the illustrations nor the interpretations of the accompanying texts. Her artwork, like that of certain non-Western artistic traditions, has little or no representative purpose. It does not, in fact, depict the mystical quest. **It is the mystical quest!**

In a passionate, sincere frame of mind, the artist has created a lyrical poem bespeaking her love for God and faith in Life. Each image is like a song expressing confidence in man's present and eternal destiny, praise for his designated role as God's companion, and yearning for a world of ideal beauty and ultimate knowledge. Jerusalem, the leitmotif of each song (even if is not always concretely represented), is a magical diaphragm. Through it, a glimpse of this ideal world of ineffable grace and sensuous order is disclosed to the onlooker. The viewer is continuously invited (the mystic always strives to communicate!) to tread on a path, the path of the Torah, which comes from and leads to Jerusalem. It is only there – in this virtual place that can be

---

19. ibid., p. 163.

20. ibid., p. 111.

everywhere, but always within the soul – that our material being becomes aware of its transcendent essence. Jerusalem is the capital of the Spiritual Life.

Does this artistic discourse have any contiguity with the main trend in contemporary art? If so, it is only in the sense that color is used in the two fields of action. In contemporary art there are not only taboo modes of expression but also taboo subjects. Contemporary art shows little interest, if any, in feeling and faith. Concerned mainly with problems of representation, relation between art and object, politics, conceptual games, and textures, the so-called avant-garde admits religious themes only if they are esoteric. Passion banished, it is no wonder that the output is often dry and scorched.

Recently, art historians claim to have found mystical themes in the work of certain modern and contemporary artists. Exhibitions were mounted, catalogues published, and an entire issue of *Art Journal* was dedicated to this topic.[21] It was much ado about nothing. These same art historians related to the presence of a few mystical motifs as if they were the equivalents of full-fledged mystical experience. When some form of mystical matter was identified, its interpretation was rooted more in cultural analysis than in religious phenomenology. Consciously or not, staggering differences in size and kind were categorically deleted.

The feeling that contemporary art lacks spirit, vitality, and direction still bothers some art people, who dare to express a desire for change. The comments of Bill Jones, artist and art journalist,[22] permit us to better position Rothenberg's mystical approach in a contemporary artistic perspective:

Art is not only a matter of inspiration and intuition, but of humility and deep introspection. If we can share our knowledge, art will once again become integrated with the life of the community at large. Deep within the order of Malkhuth, devoid of God's light, art's mystery is invested in the material world. But who will empower this art of human endeavor? Spiritual vision is not exclusive. A renewal, redeeming knowledge must fill the good works. The biblical lesson of the graven image is clear; as the choice between the Trees of Life and Knowledge again presents itself, we are to understand the consequences and choose life.

Dan Eban
Jerusalem, August 1995

---

21. Art Journal 46:1 (Spring 1987).

22. Bill Jones, "Graven Images," Arts Magazine 63:9 (May 1989), pp. 73–77.

Pray for the peace of Jerusalem.

שַׁאֲלוּ שְׁלוֹם יְרוּשָׁלִָם.

 **Let there be light**

ויאמר אלהים יהי-אור ויהי-אור: וירא אלהים את-האור כי-טוב ויבדל אלהים
בין האור ובין החשך.
בראשית א:ג-ד

And God said, Let there be light: and there was light. And
God saw the light, that it was good: and God divided the light
from the darkness.
Genesis 1:3-4

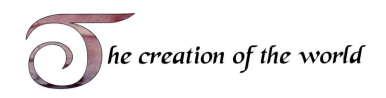

The creation of the world

ריאת העולם

בדבר יהוה שמים נעשו וברוח פיו כל-צבאם.

תהלים לג:ו

מציון מכלל-יפי אלהים הופיע.

תהלים נ:ב

By the word of the Lord were the heavens made; and all the
host of them by the breath of his mouth.

Psalms 33:6

Out of Zion, the perfection of beauty, God has shone forth.

Psalms 50:2

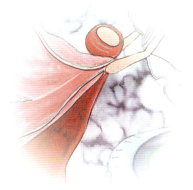

Riky Rothenberg

ויאמר אלהים נעשה אדם בצלמנו כדמותנו... ויברא אלהים את-האדם בצלמו
בצלם אלהים ברא אתו זכר ונקבה ברא אתם: ויברך אתם אלהים ויאמר
להם אלהים פרו ורבו ומלאו את-הארץ וכבשה.
בראשית א:כו-כח

And God said, Let us make Mankind in our image, after our
likeness... So God created Mankind in his own image, in the
image of God he created him; male and female he created them.
And God blessed them, and God said to them, Be fruitful, and
multiply, replenish the earth, and subdue it.
Genesis 1:26-28

גדול יהוה ומהלל מאד בעיר אלהינו הר-קדשו: יפה נוף משוש כל-הארץ
הר-ציון ירכתי צפון קרית מלך רב: אלהים בארמנותיה נודע למשגב:
כאשר שמענו כן ראינו בעיר יהוה-צבאות בעיר אלהינו אלהים יכוננה עד-עולם
סלה.

תהלים מח:ב-ג, ט

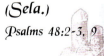

Great is the Lord, and highly to be praised in the city of our
God, in the mountain of his holiness. Beautiful for situation,
the joy of the whole earth: mount Zion, the sides of the north,
the city of the great King. God is known in her palaces for a
fortress.

As we have heard, so have we seen in the city of the Lord of
hosts, in the city of our God: may God establish it for ever.
(Sela.)

Psalms 48:2-3, 9

 he flood

 מבול

והקמתי את-בריתי אתכם ולא-יכרת כל-בשר עוד ממי המבול ולא-יהיה עוד
מבול לשחת הארץ:
את-קשתי נתתי בענן והיתה לאות ברית ביני ובין הארץ: והיה בענני ענן
על-הארץ ונראתה הקשת בענן.

בראשית ט:יא, יג-יד

And I will establish my covenant with you; neither shall all
flesh be cut off any more by the waters of the flood; neither
shall there any more be a flood to destroy the earth.
I have set my bow in the cloud, and it shall be for a token of
a covenant between me and the earth. And it shall come to pass,
when I bring a cloud over the earth, that the bow shall be seen
in the cloud.

Genesis 9:11, 13-14

והיה שמך אברהם כי אב-המון גוים נתתיך: והפרתי אתך במאד מאד ונתתיך
לגוים ומלכים ממך יצאו:

ונתתי לך ולזרעך אחריך את ארץ מגריך את כל-ארץ כנען לאחזת עולם והייתי
להם לאלהים:

שרי אשתך לא-תקרא את-שמה שרי כי שרה שמה: וברכתי אתה וגם נתתי ממנה
לך בן וברכתיה והיתה לגוים מלכי עמים ממנה יהיו.

בראשית יז:ה-ו, ח, טו-טז

Thy name shall be Abraham; for a father of many nations have
I made thee. And I will make thee exceedingly fruitful, and I
will make nations of thee, and kings shall come out of thee.
And I will give to thee, and to thy seed after thee, the land in
which thou dost sojourn, all the land of Canaan, for an
everlasting possession; and I will be their God.
As for Saray thy wife, thou shalt not call her name Saray,
but Sarah shall her name be. And I will bless her, and give
thee a son also of her; and I will bless her, and she shall be a
mother of nations; kings of peoples shall issue from her.
Genesis 17:5-6, 8, 15-16

 he twins

 תאומים

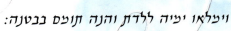

וימלאו ימיה ללדת והנה תומם בבטנה:
ויגדלו הנערים ויהי עשו איש ידע ציד איש שדה ויעקב איש תם ישב
אהלים: ויאהב יצחק את-עשו כי-ציד בפיו ורבקה אהבת את-יעקב.
בראשית כה:כד, כז-כח

And when her days to be delivered were fulfilled, behold, there were twins in her womb.

And the boys grew: and 'Esau was a cunning hunter, a man of the field; and Jacob was a plain man, dwelling in tents. And Isaac loved 'Esau, for he relished his venison: but Rebekah loved Jacob.

Genesis 25:24, 27-28

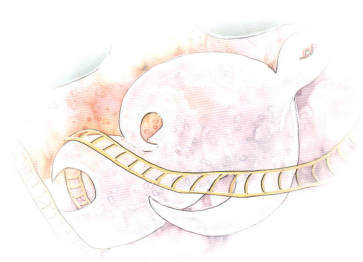

ויקרא יצחק אל-יעקב ויברך אתו ויצוהו ויאמר לו לא-תקח אשה מבנות כנען:
ואל שדי יברך אתך ויפרך וירבך והיית לקהל עמים: ויתן-לך את-ברכת אברהם
לך ולזרעך אתך לרשתך את-ארץ מגריך אשר-נתן אלהים לאברהם.
בראשית כח:א, ג-ד

And Isaac called Jacob, and blessed him, and charged him, and
said to him, Thou shalt not take a wife of the daughters of
Canaan.
And God Almighty bless thee, and make thee fruitful, and
multiply thee, that thou mayst be a multitude of people; and give
thee the blessing of Abraham, to thee, and to thy seed with thee;
that thou mayst inherit the land in which thou art a sojourner,
and which God gave to Abraham.
Genesis 28:1, 3-4

ויפגע במקום וילן שם כי-בא השמש ויקח מאבני המקום וישם מראשתיו
וישכב במקום ההוא: ויחלם והנה סלם מצב ארצה וראשו מגיע השמימה
והנה מלאכי אלהים עלים וירדים בו: והנה יהוה נצב עליו ויאמר אני יהוה
אלהי אברהם אביך ואלהי יצחק הארץ אשר אתה שכב עליה לך אתננה
ולזרעך.

בראשית כח:יא-יג

And he lighted on a certain place, and tarried there all night,
because the sun was set; and he took of the stones of that place,
and put them under his head, and lay down in that place to
sleep. And he dreamed, and behold a ladder set up on the earth,
and the top of it reached to heaven: and behold the angels of
God ascending and descending on it. And, behold, the Lord
stood above it, and said, I am the Lord God of Abraham thy
father, and the God of Isaac; the land on which thou liest, to
thee will I give it, and to thy seed.

Genesis 28:11-13

Jacob wrestling with the angel

אבק יעקב עם המלאך

ויותר יעקב לבדו ויאבק איש עמו עד עלות השחר: וירא כי לא יכל לו ויגע
בכף-ירכו ותקע כף-ירך יעקב בהאבקו עמו: ויאמר שלחני כי עלה השחר
ויאמר לא אשלחך כי אם-ברכתני: ויאמר אליו מה-שמך ויאמר יעקב: ויאמר
לא יעקב יאמר עוד שמך כי אם-ישראל כי-שרית עם-אלהים ועם-אנשים
ותוכל.

בראשית לב:כה-כט

And Jacob was left alone; and there wrestled a man with him
until the breaking of the day. And when he saw that he did not
prevail against him, he touched the hollow of his thigh; and the
hollow of Jacob's thigh was put out of joint, as he wrestled
with him. And he said, Let me go, for the say breaks. And he
said, I will not let thee go, unless thou bless me. And he said
to him, What is thy name? And he said, Jacob. And he said,
Thy name shall be called no more Jacob, but Israel: for thou
hast contended with God and with men, and hast prevailed.
Genesis 32:25-29

Joseph and his brothers

ויאמר יוסף אל-אחיו אני יוסף העוד אבי חי ולא-יכלו אחיו לענות אתו כי
נבהלו מפניו: ויאמר יוסף אל-אחיו גשו-נא אלי ויגשו ויאמר אני יוסף אחיכם
אשר-מכרתם אתי מצרימה.

בראשית מה:ג-ד

ויפל על-צוארי בנימן-אחיו ויבך ובנימן בכה על-צואריו: וינשק לכל-אחיו
ויבך עלהם ואחרי כן דברו אחיו אתו.

בראשית מה:יד-טו

And Joseph said to his brethren, I am Joseph: does my father
yet live? And his brothers could not answer him; for they were
terrified at his presence. And Joseph said to his brothers, Come
near to me, I pray you. And they came near. And he said, I
am Joseph your brother, whom you sold into Egypt.
Genesis 45:3-4

An he fell on his brother Benjanim's neck, and wept; and
Benjanim wept on his neck. And he kissed all his brethren, and
wept on them; and after that his brethren talked with him.
Genesis 45:14-15

וישלח ישראל את-ימינו וישת על-ראש אפרים והוא הצעיר ואת-שמאלו
על-ראש מנשה שכל את-ידיו כי מנשה הבכור.
בראשית מח:יד

ויקרא יעקב אל-בניו ויאמר האספו ואגידה לכם את אשר-יקרא אתכם באחרית
הימים: הקבצו ושמעו בני יעקב ושמעו אל-ישראל אביכם.
בראשית מט:א-ב

And Israel stretched out his right hand, and laid it upon Ephraim's
head, who was the younger, and his left hand upon Manasseh's head,
changing his hands; for Manasseh was the first-born.
Genesis 48:14

And Jacob called to his sons, and said, Gather yourselves together,
that I may tell you that which shall befall you in the last days. Gather
yourselves together, and hear, you sons of Jacob; and hearken to
Israel your father.
Genesis 49:1-2

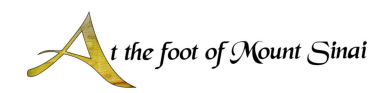 

At the foot of Mount Sinai

ויוצא משה את-העם לקראת האלהים מן-המחנה ויתיצבו בתחתית ההר.

שמות יט:יז

ויהי ברדת משה מהר סיני ושני לחת העדת ביד-משה ברדתו מן-ההר ומשה
לא-ידע כי קרן עור פניו בדברו אתו.

שמות לד:כט

And Moses brought the people out of the camp to meet with
God; and they stood at the foot of the mountain.
Exodus 19:17

And it came to pass, when Moses came down from Mount
Sinai with the two tablets of Testimony in Moses' hand, when
he came down from the mountain, that Moses knew not that
the skin of his face shone while he talked with him.
Exodus 34:29

 **David & Jonathan**

דוד ויהונתן

ונפש יהונתן נקשרה בנפש דוד ויאהבו יהונתן כנפשו: ויכרת יהונתן ודוד
ברית באהבתו אתו כנפשו.

שמואל א' יח:א,ג

And it came to pass... that the soul of Jonathan was knit with
the soul of David, and Jonathan loved him as his own soul.
Then Jonathan and David made a convenant, because he loved
him as his own soul.

1 Samuel 18:1, 3

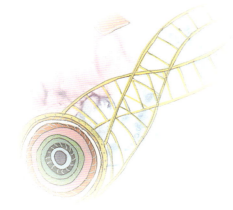

 David & Bathsheba

 דוד ובת-שבע

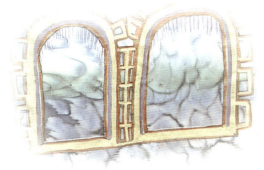

ויהי לעת הערב ויקם דוד מעל משכבו ויתהלך על-גג בית-המלך וירא אשה
רחצת מעל הגג והאשה טובת מראה מאד: וישלח דוד וידרש לאשה ויאמר
הלוא-זאת בת-שבע בת-אליעם אשת אוריה החתי: וישלח דוד מלאכים
ויקחה ותבוא אליו וישכב עמה.

שמואל ב' יא:ב-ד

And it came to pass one evening, that David arose from his
bed, and walked upon the roof of the king's house: and from the
roof he saw a woman bathing; and the woman was very fair
to look upon. And David sent and inquired after the woman.
And one said, Is not this Bathsheba, the daughter of Eliam,
the wife of Uriah the Hittite? And David sent messengers,
and took her; and she came in to him, and he lay with her.

2 Samuel 11:2-4

Ribeca N.D.B

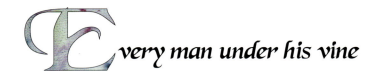 

Every man under his vine   איש תחת גפנו

יהודה וישראל רבים כחול אשר-על-הים לרב אכלים ושתים ושמחים.

מלכים א' ד:כ

ושלמה היה מושל בכל-הממלכות מן-הנהר ארץ פלשתים ועד גבול מצרים
מגשים מנחה ועבדים את שלמה כל-ימי חייו:
וישב יהודה וישראל לבטח איש תחת גפנו ותחת תאנתו מדן ועד-באר שבע
כל ימי שלמה.

מלכים א' ה:א, ה

*Judah and Israel were many, as the sand which by the sea for
multitude; they ate, and drank, and were happy.*
1 Kings 4:20

*And Solomon reigned over all kindoms from the river to the
land of the Philistines, and to the border of Egypt.*
*And Judah and Israel dwelt in safety, every man under his
vine and under his fig tree, from Dan to Beersheba, all the
days of Solomon.*
1 Kings 5:1, 5

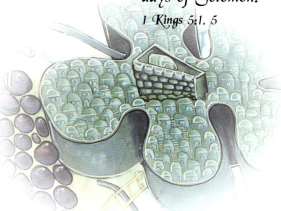

 The golden days of Solomon

 ריחה בימי שלמה

הנה עשיתי כדבריך הנה נתתי לך לב חכם ונבון אשר כמוך לא-היה לפניך
ואחריך לא-יקום כמוך: וגם אשר לא-שאלת נתתי לך גם-עשר גם-כבוד אשר
לא-היה כמוך איש במלכים כל-ימיך.

מלכים א' ג:יב-יג

Behold, I have done according to thy words: lo, I have given
thee a wise and an understanding heart; so that there has been
none like thee before thee, nor after thee shall any arise like
thee. And I have also given thee that which thou hast not asked,
both riches and honour: so that there shall not be any among the
kings like thee all thy days.

1 Kings 3:12-13

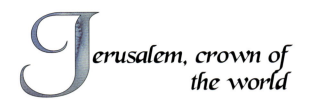

Jerusalem, crown of the world

כֶּתֶר לְעוֹלָם
יְרוּשָׁלַיִם

וְהָיָה בְּאַחֲרִית הַיָּמִים נָכוֹן יִהְיֶה הַר בֵּית-יְהוָה בְּרֹאשׁ הֶהָרִים וְנִשָּׂא מִגְּבָעוֹת
וְנָהֲרוּ אֵלָיו כָּל-הַגּוֹיִם: וְהָלְכוּ עַמִּים רַבִּים וְאָמְרוּ לְכוּ וְנַעֲלֶה אֶל-הַר-יְהוָה
אֶל-בֵּית אֱלֹהֵי יַעֲקֹב וְיוֹרֵנוּ מִדְּרָכָיו וְנֵלְכָה בְּאֹרְחֹתָיו כִּי מִצִּיּוֹן תֵּצֵא תוֹרָה
וּדְבַר-יְהוָה מִירוּשָׁלָיִם: וְשָׁפַט בֵּין הַגּוֹיִם וְהוֹכִיחַ לְעַמִּים רַבִּים וְכִתְּתוּ חַרְבוֹתָם
לְאִתִּים וַחֲנִיתוֹתֵיהֶם לְמַזְמֵרוֹת לֹא-יִשָּׂא גוֹי אֶל-גּוֹי חֶרֶב וְלֹא-יִלְמְדוּ עוֹד מִלְחָמָה.
יְשַׁעְיָה ב:ב-ד

And it shall come to pass in the last days, that the mountain of the Lord's house shall be established on the top of the mountains, and shall be exalted above the hills; and all the nations shall flow unto it. And many people shall go and say, Come, and let us go up to the mountain of the Lord's, to the house of the God of Jacob; and he will teach us of his ways, and we will walk in his paths: for out of Zion shall go forth Torah, and the word of the Lord's from Jerusalem. And he shall judge among the nations, and shall decide among many people: and they shall beat their swords into plowshares, and their spears into pruning hooks: nation shall not lift up sword against nation, neither shall they learn war any more.

Isaiah 2:2-4

 Light for all

 אור לחבל

קומי אורי כי בא אורך וכבוד יהוה עליך זרח: כי-הנה החשך יכסה-ארץ
וערפל לאמים ועליך יזרח יהוה וכבודו עליך יראה: והלכו גוים לאורך ומלכים
לנגה זרחך.

ישעיה ס:א-ג

Arise, shine, for thy light is come, and the glory of the Lord is
risen upon thee. For, behold, the darkness shall cover the earth,
and gross darkness the peoples: but the Lord shall arise upon
thee, and his glory shall be seen upon thee. And nations shall
walk at thy light, and kings at the brightness of thy rising.
Isaiah 60:1-3

הנה אל ישועתי אבטח ולא אפחד כי-עזי וזמרת יה יהוה ויהי-לי לישועה:
ושאבתם-מים בששון ממעיני הישועה: ואמרתם ביום ההוא הודו ליהוה
קראו בשמו הודיעו בעמים עלילתיו הזכירו כי נשגב שמו: זמרו יהוה כי
גאות עשה מודעת זאת בכל-הארץ: צהלי ורני יושבת ציון כי-גדול בקרבך
קדוש ישראל.

ישעיה יב:ב-ו

Behold, God is my salvation; I will trust, and not be afraid:
for the Lord God is my strength and my song... Therefore with
joy shall you draw water out of the wells of salvation. And in
that day shall you say, Praise the Lord, call upon his name,
declare his doings among the people, make mention that his name
is exalted. Sing to the Lord; for he has done excellent things:
this is known in all the earth. Cry out and shout, thou inhabitant
of Zion: for great is the Holy One of Israel in the midst of
thee.

Isaiah 12:2-6

The love festival in Jerusalem

עות ירושלים
בחג האהבה

כשושנה בין החוחים כן רעיתי בין הבנות.
שיר השירים ב:ב

זה דודי וזה רעי בנות ירושלם.
שיר השירים ה:טז

Like the lily among thorns, so is my love among the daughters.
Song of Songs 2:2

This is my beloved, and this is my friend, O daughters of Jerusalem.
Song of Songs 5:16

Love song to Jerusalem

שיר אהבה לירושלים

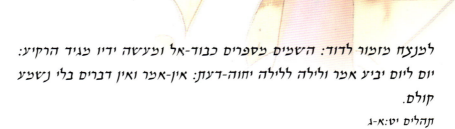

למנצח מזמור לדוד: השמים מספרים כבוד-אל ומעשה ידיו מגיד הרקיע: יום ליום יביע אמר ולילה ללילה יחוה-דעת: אין-אמר ואין דברים בלי נשמע קולם.

תהלים יט:א-ג

To the chief Musician, A Psalm of David. The heavens declare the glory of God; and the firmament proclaims his handiwork. Day to day utters speech, and night to night expresses knowledge. There is no speech nor are there words; their voice is not heard.

Psalms 19:1-3

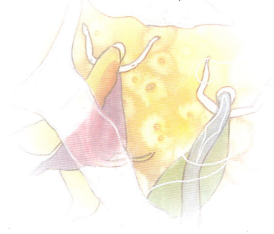

איכה ישבה בדד העיר רבתי עם היתה כאלמנה רבתי בגוים שרתי במדינות
היתה למס: בכו תבכה בלילה ודמעתה על לחיה אין-לה מנחם מכל-אהביה
כל-רעיה בגדו בה היו לה לאיבים.

איכה א:א-ב

How does the city sit solitary, that was full of people! How
is she become like a widow! she that was great among the
nations, and princess among the provinces, how is she beome a
vassal! She weeps sore in the night, and her tears are on her
cheeks: among all her lovers she has none to comfort her: all
her friends have dealt treacherously with her, they have become
her enemies.

Lamentations 1:1-2

 On Mount Zion

עַל-זֶה הָיָה דָוֶה לִבֵּנוּ עַל-אֵלֶּה חָשְׁכוּ עֵינֵינוּ: עַל הַר-צִיּוֹן שֶׁשָּׁמֵם שׁוּעָלִים
הִלְּכוּ-בוֹ: אַתָּה יְהוָה לְעוֹלָם תֵּשֵׁב כִּסְאֲךָ לְדֹר וָדוֹר: לָמָּה לָנֶצַח תִּשְׁכָּחֵנוּ
תַּעַזְבֵנוּ לְאֹרֶךְ יָמִים: הֲשִׁיבֵנוּ יְהוָה אֵלֶיךָ וְנָשׁוּבָ חַדֵּשׁ יָמֵינוּ כְּקֶדֶם: כִּי אִם-מָאֹס
מְאַסְתָּנוּ קָצַפְתָּ עָלֵינוּ עַד-מְאֹד.

איכה ה:יז-כב

For this our heart is faint; for these things our eyes are dim.
Because of the Mount of Zion, which is desolate, foxes prowl
over it. Thou, O Lord, art enthroned forever; thy throne is
from generation to generation. Why dost thou forget us forever,
why dost thou so long forsake us? Turn us to thee, O Lord,
and we shall be turned; renew our days as of old; unless thou
hast utterly rejected us; and art exceedingly angry against us.

Lamentations 5:17-22

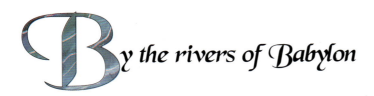 

By the rivers of Babylon

ל נהרות בבל

על־נהרות בבל שם ישבנו גם־בכינו בזכרנו את־ציון: אם־אשכחך ירושלם
תשכח ימיני: תדבק לשוני לחכי אם־לא אזכרכי אם־לא אעלה את־ירושלם
על ראש שמחתי.

תהלים קלז:א, ה-ו

By the rivers of Babylon, there we sat down, yea, we wept, when we
remembered Zion. If I forget thee, O Jerusalem, let my right hand forget
her cunning. If I do not remember thee, let my tongue cleave to the roof
of my mouth; if I do not set Jerusalem above my highest joy.

Psalms 137:1, 5-6

 he Hasmonean wars

 לחמות חשמונאים

יונים נקבצו עלי אזי בימי חשמנים' ופרצו חומות מגדלי וטמאו כל השמנים'
ומנותר קנקנים נעשה נס לשושנים' בני בינה ימי שמונה קבעו שיר ורננים.
חשוף זרוע קדשך וקרב קץ הישועה' נקום נקמת דם עבדיך מאמה הרשעה'
כי ארכה לנו הישועה ואין קץ לימי הרעה' דחה אדמון בצל צלמון הקם
לנו רועים שבעה.

"מעוז צור"

Greeks gathered against me then in Hasmonean days. They
breached the walls of my towers and they defiled all the oils;
And from the one remnant of the flasks a miracle was wrought
for the roses. Men of insight – eight days established for song
and jubilation.
Bare Your holy arm and hasten the End for salvation – Avenge
the vengeance of Your servant's blood from the wicked nation.
For the triumph is too long delayed for us, and there is no end
to days of evil. Repel the Red One in the nethermost shadow
and establish for us the seven shepherds.
From "Maoz Tzur" (O mighty Rock)

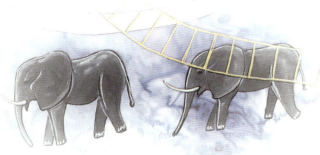

A glimpse of light

ש בב אור

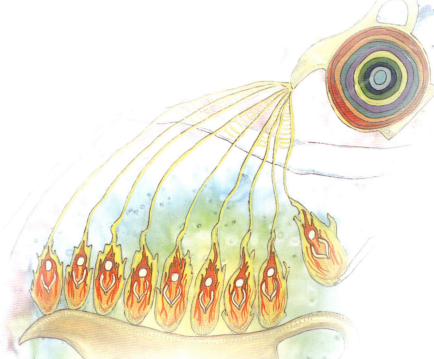

הנרות הללו אנחנו מדליקין על הנסים ועל הנפלאות ועל התשועות ועל המלחמות
שעשית לאבותינו בימים ההם בזמן הזה, על ידי כהניך הקדושים. וכל שמונת ימי
חנוכה, הנרות הללו קדש הם. ואין לנו רשות להשתמש בהם, אלא לראותם בלבד,
כדי להודות ולהלל לשמך הגדול על נסיך ועל נפלאותיך ועל ישועתך.

הנרות הללו – מתוך התפילה

These lights we kindle upon the miracles, the wonders, the
salvations, and the battles which you performed for our
forefathers in those days at this season through Your holy priests.
During all eight days of Hanukkah these lights are sacred, and
we are not permitted to make ordinary use of them, but to look
at them in order to express thanks and praise to Your great Name
for Your miracles, Your wonders, and Your salvations.

"These Lights" from the Hanukkah blessing

למען ציון לא אחשה ולמען ירושלם לא אשקוט עד-יצא כנגה צדקה וישועתה
כלפיד יבער: וראו גוים צדקך וכל-מלכים כבודך וקרא לך שם חדש אשר
פי יהוה יקבנו: והיית עטרת תפארת ביד-יהוה וצנוף מלוכה בכף-אלהיך.

ישעיה סב:א-ג

For the sake of Zion I will not hold my peace, and for the
sake of Jerusalem, I will not be still, until her righteousness
goes forth like radiance, and her salvation like a burning torch.
And the nations shall see thy righteousness, and all kings thy
glory: and thou shalt be called by a new name, which the mouth
of the Lord shall express. Thou shalt also be a crown of glory
in the hand of the Lord, and a royal diadem in the hand of thy
God.

Isaiah 62:1-3

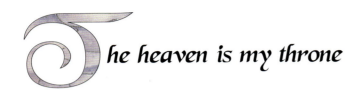 he heaven is my throne

 שמים כסאי

כה אמר יהוה השמים כסאי והארץ הדם רגלי אי־זה בית אשר תבנו־לי
ואי־זה מקום מנוחתי.

ישעיה סו:א

עשמים הביט יהוה ראה את־כל־בני האדם: ממכון־שבתו השגיח אל כל־ישבי
הארץ.

תהלים לג:יג־יד

Thus says the Lord, The heaven is my throne, and the earth is
my footstool: where is the house that you would build for me?
and where is the place of my rest?

Isaiah 66:1

The Lord looks down from heaven; he beholds all the sons of
men. From the place of his habitation he looks upon all the
inhabitants of the earth.

Psalms 33:13-14

 Psalm of David

 זמור לדוד

למנצח על אילת השחר מזמור לדוד: אלי אלי למה עזבתני רחוק מישועתי דברי
שאגתי: אלהי אקרא יומם ולא תענה ולילה ולא-דומיה לי.

תהלים כב:א-ג

To the chief Musician upon Ayyelet-hashshahar, A Psalm of
David. My God, my God, why hast thou forasken me? why
art thou so far from helping me, from the words of my loud
complaint? O my God, I cry in the daytime, but thou hearest
not; and in the night season, and I have no rest.

Psalms 22:1-3

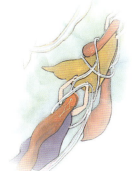

 raise to the Lord

בחי ירושלים

שבחי ירושלם את-יהוה הללי אלהיך ציון: כי-חזק בריחי שעריך ברך בניך
בקרבך: השם-גבולך שלום חלב חטים ישביעך: השלח אמרתו ארץ עד-מהרה
ירוץ דברו: הנתן שלג כצמר כפור כאפר יפזר: משליך קרחו כפתים לפני
קרתו מי יעמד: ישלח דברו וימסם ישב רוחו יזלו-מים: מגיד דברו ליעקב
חקיו ומשפטיו לישראל.

תהלים קמז:יב-יט

Praise the Lord, O Jerusalem; praise thy God, O Zion. For
he has strengthened the bars of thy gates; he has blessed thy
children within thee. He makes peace in thy borders, and fills
thee with the finest of the wheat. He sends forth his
commandment upon the earth: his word runs very swiftly. He
gives snow like wool: he scatters the hoar frost like ashes. He
casts forth his ice like morsels: who can stand before his cold?
He sends out his word, and melts them: he causes his wind to
blow: they run as water. He declares his Word to Jacob, his
statutes and his judgments to Israel.

Psalms 147:12-19

 **Daybreak**

העם ההלכים בחשך ראו אור גדול ישבי בארץ צלמות אור נגה עליהם: הרבית הגוי
לא הגדלת השמחה שמחו לפניך כשמחת בקציר כאשר יגילו בחלקם שלל: כי את-על
סבלו ואת מטה שכמו שבט הנגש בו החתת כיום מדין.

ישעיה ט:א-ג

The people that walked in darkness have seen a great light:
they that dwelt in the land of the shadow of death, upon them
has the light shone. Thou hast multiplied the nation, and
increased their joy: they joy before thee according to the joy in
harvest, and as men rejoice when they divide the spoil. For
thou hast broken the yoke of his burden, and the staff of his
shoulder, the rod of his oppressor, as in the day of Midian.
Isaiah 9:1-3

Gathering the Diaspora

 קיבוץ גליות

אל-תירא כי-אתך אני ממזרח אביא זרעך וממערב אקבצך: אמר לצפון תני ולתימן
אל-תכלאי הביאי בני מרחוק ובנותי מקצה הארץ.

ישעיה מג:ה-ו

כרעה עדרו ירעה בזרעו יקבץ טלאים ובחיקו ישא עלות ינהל.

ישעיה מ:יא

Fear not: for I am with thee: I will bring they seed from the
east, and gather thee from the west; I will say to the north,
Give up; and to the south, Keep not back: bring my sons from
far, and my daughters from the ends of the earth.
Isaiah 43:5-6

He shall feed his flock like a shepherd: he shall gather the lambs
with his arm, and carry them in his bosom, and shall gently lead
those that are with young.
Isaiah 40:11

 he dove

 יונה

וקוי יהוה יחליפו כח יעלו אבר כנשרים ירוצו ולא ייגעו ילכו ולא ייעפו.

ישעיה מ:לא

ופדויי יהוה ישובון ובאו ציון ברנה ושמחת עולם על-ראשם ששון ושמחה
ישיגון נסו יגון ואנחה.

ישעיה נא:יא

But they that wait upon the Lord shall renew their strength;
they shall mount up with wings as eagles; they shall run, and
not be weary; they shall walk, and not faint.

Isaiah 40:31

Therefore the redeemed of the Lord shall return, and come
with singing to Zion; and everlasting joy shall be upon their
head; they shall obtain gladness and joy; and sorrow and sighing
shall flee away.

Isaiah 51:11

 he reunited city

שיר המעלות לדוד שמחתי באמרים לי בית יהוה נלך: עמדות היו רגלינו
בשעריך ירושלם: ירושלם הבנויה כעיר שחברה-לה יחדו: ששם עלו שבטים
שבטי-יה עדות לישראל להדות לשם יהוה: כי שמה ישבו כסאות למשפט
כסאות לבית דוד: שאלו שלום ירושלם ישליו אהביך: יהי-שלום בחילך
שלוה בארמנותיך: למען אחי ורעי אדברה-נא שלום בך: למען בית-יהוה
אלהינו אבקשה טוב לך.

תהלים קכב

A Song of Ascents, of David. I was glad when they said to
me, let us go into the house of the Lord: when our feet stood
within thy gates, O Jerusalem: O Jerusalem, built as a city
that is compact together: there the tribes used to go up, the tribes
of the Lord, an appointed practice for Israel, to give thanks to
the name of the Lord. For there are set thrones of judgment,
the thones of the house of David. Pray for the peace of
Jerusalem: they who love thee shall prosper: peace be within
thy walls, and prosperity within thy palaces. For my brethren
and companions' sakes, I will now say, Peace be within thee.
For the sake of the house of the Lord our God I will seek thy
good.

Psalms 122

 # A gate to the city

 עיר ירושלים

שאו שערים ראשיכם והנשאו פתחי עולם ויבוא מלך הכבוד: מי זה מלך
הכבוד יהוה עזוז וגבור יהוה גבור מלחמה: שאו שערים ראשיכם ושאו
פתחי עולם ויבא מלך הכבוד: מי הוא זה מלך הכבוד יהוה צבאות הוא
מלך הכבוד סלה.

תהלים כד:ז-י

Lift up your heads, O you gates; and be lifted up, you
everlasting doors; and the King of glory shall come in. Who is
this King of glory? The Lord strong and mighty, the Lord
mighty in battle. Lift up your heads, O you gates; and lift them
up, you everlasting doors; that the King of glory may come in.
Who is this King of glory? The Lord of hosts, he is the King
of glory. (Sela.)

Psalms 24:7-10

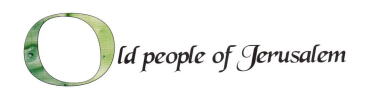 **O**ld people of Jerusalem

 קנים וזקנות בירושלים

כה אמר יהוה צבאות עד ישבו זקנים וזקנות ברחבות ירושלם ואיש משענתו
בידו מרב ימים: ורחבות העיר ימלאו ילדים וילדות משחקים ברחבתיה: כה
אמר יהוה צבאות כי יפלא בעיני שארית העם הזה בימים ההם גם-בעיני
יפלא נאם יהוה צבאות.

זכריה ח:ד-ו

Thus says the Lord of Hosts; Old men and old women shall
yet again dwell in the streets of Jerusalem, and every man
with his staff in his hand for very age. And the streets of the
city shall be full of boys and girls playing in its streets. Thus
says the Lord of hosts; If it be marvellous in the eyes of the
remnant of this people in these days, it will also be marvellous
in my eyes, says the Lord of hosts.
Zechariah 8:4-6

 **Mevasseret Yerushalayim**

 בשרת ירושלים

על הר-גבה עלי-לך מבשרת ציון הרימי בכח קולך מבשרת ירושלם הרימי
אל-תיראי אמרי לערי יהודה הנה אלהיכם: הנה אדני יהוה בחזק יבוא
וזרעו משלה לו הנה שכרו אתו ופעלתו לפניו.

ישעיה מ:ט-י

Thou that bringest good tidings to Zion, get thee up into the
high mountain; Thou that bringest good tidings to Jerusalem,
lift up thy voice with strength; lift it up, be not afraid; say to
the cities of Judah, Behold your God! Behold, the Lord God
will come with might, and his arm shall rule for him; behold,
his reward is with him, And his hire before him.
Isaiah 40:9-10

75-pl. 38

ow beautiful upon the mountains

מה נאו על
ההרים

מה-נָאווּ עַל-הֶהָרִים רַגְלֵי מְבַשֵׂר מַשְׁמִיעַ שָׁלוֹם מְבַשֵׂר טוֹב מַשְׁמִיעַ יְשׁוּעָה
אֹמֵר לְצִיּוֹן מָלַךְ אֱלֹהָיִךְ: קוֹל צֹפַיִךְ נָשְׂאוּ קוֹל יַחְדָּו יְרַנֵּנוּ כִּי עַיִן בְּעַיִן יִרְאוּ
בְּשׁוּב יְהוָה צִיּוֹן: פִּצְחוּ רַנְּנוּ יַחְדָּו חָרְבוֹת יְרוּשָׁלִָם כִּי-נִחַם יְהוָה עַמּוֹ גָּאַל
יְרוּשָׁלִָם.

ישעיה נב:ז-ט

How beautiful upon the mountains are the feet of him that
brings good tidings, that announces peace; that brings good tidings
of good, that announces salvation; that says to Zion, Thy God
reigns! The voice of thy watchmen is heard: they lift up the
voice; together shall they sing: for they shall see eye to eye, the
Lord returning to Zion. Break forth into joy, sing together, O
waste places of Jerusalem: for the Lord has comforted his
people, he has redeemed Jerusalem.

Isaiah 52:7-9

 **Peace**

 שלום

פתחו שערים ויבא גוי-צדיק שמר אמנים: יצר סמוך תצר שלום שלום כי בך

בטוח: בטחו ביהוה עדי-עד כי ביה יהוה צור עולמים.

ישעיה כו:ב-ד

או יחזק במעזי יעשה שלום לי שלום יעשה-לי: הבאים ישרש יעקב יציץ

ופרח ישראל ומלאו פני-תבל תנובה.

ישעיה כז:ה-ו

Open the gates, that the righteous nation that keeps faithfulness
may enter in: Thou wilt keep him in perfect peace, whose mind
is stayed on thee: because he trusts in thee. Trust in the Lord
for ever: for the Lord God is an eternal Rock.
Isaiah 26:2-4

Or let him take hold of my strength, that he may make peace
with me; and he shall make peace with me. In days to come
Jacob shall take root: Israel shall blossom and bud, and the face
of the world shall be filled with fruit.
Isaiah 27:5-6

Peace like a river

נהר שלום

כי-כה אמר יהוה הנני נטה-אליה כנהר שלום וכנחל שוטף כבוד גוים וינקתם
על-צד תנשאו ועל-ברכים תשעשעו: כאיש אשר אמו תנחמנו כן אנכי אנחמכם
ובירושלם תנחמו: וראיתם ושש לבכם ועצמותיכם כדשא תפרחנה ונודעה
יד-יהוה את-עבדיו וזעם את-איביו.

ישעיה סו:יב-יד

For thus says the Lord, Behold, I will extend peace to her
like a river, and the glory of the nations like a flowing stream:
then shall you suck, you shall be carried upon her sides, and be
dandled upon her knees. As one whom his mother comforts, so
will I comfort you; and you shall be comforted in Jerusalem.
And when you see this, your heart shall rejoice, and your bones
shall flourish like grass: and the hand of the Lord shall be known
toward his servants, and his indignation toward his enemies.

Isaiah 66:12-14

The Sabbath in Jerusalem

בת ירושלים

כה אמר יהוה שמרו משפט ועשו צדקה כי-קרובה ישועתי לבוא וצדקתי

להגלות: אשרי אנוש יעשה-זאת ובן-אדם יחזיק בה שמר שבת מחללו ושמר

ידו מעשות כל-רע.

ישעיה נו:א-ב

Thus says the Lord, Keep judgment, and do justice: for my
salvation is near to come, and my righteousness to be revealed.
Happy is the man that does this, and the son of man that lays
hold on it; that keeps the Sabbath and does not profane it, and
keeps his hand from doing any evil.

Isaiah 56:1-2

Rebeca N.D.R.

רבקה

 **I**n green pastures

נאות דשא

מזמור לדוד יהוה רעי לא אחסר: בנאות דשא ירביצני על-מי מנחות ינהלני:
נפשי ישובב ינחני במעגלי-צדק למען שמו: גם כי-אלך בגיא צלמות לא-אירא
רע כי-אתה עמדי שבטך ומשענתך המה ינחמני: תערך לפני שלחן נגד צררי
דשנת בשמן ראשי כוסי רויה: אך טוב וחסד ירדפוני כל-ימי חיי ושבתי
בבית-יהוה לארך ימים.

תהלים כג

A Psalm of David. The Lord is my shepherd; I shall not want.
He makes me to lie down in green pastures: he leads me beside
the still waters. He restores my soul: he leads me in the paths
of righteousness for his name's sake. Even though I walk
through the valley of the shadow of death, I will fear no evil:
for thou art with me; thy rod and thy staff they comfort me.
Thou preparest a table before me in the presence of my enemies:
thou anointest my head with oil; my cup runs over. Surely
goodness and mercy shall follow me all the days of my life: and
I will dwell in the house of the Lord forever.

Psalms 23

אז יבקע כשחר אורך וארכתך מהרה תצמח והלך לפניך צדקך כבוד יהוה
יאספך.

ישעיה נח:ח

Then shall thy light break forth like the morning, and thy health
shall spring forth speedily: and thy righteousness shall go before
thee; the glory of the Lord shall be thy rear guard.

Isaiah 58:8

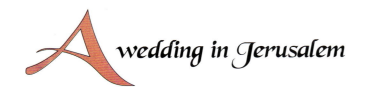 A wedding in Jerusalem

 חתונה בירושלים

ברוך אתה יהוה מלך העולם אשר ברא ששון ושמחה. חתן וכלה גילה רנה
דיצה וחדוה אהבה ואחוה ושלום ורעות. מהרה יהוה אלוהינו ישמע בערי
יהודה ובחוצות ירושלים קול ששון וקול שמחה קול חתן וקול כלה, קול
מצהלות חתנים מחפתם ונערים ממשתה נגינתם ברוך אתה יהוה משמח
חתן עם כלה.

מתוך ברכות הנשואין

Blessed are you, the Lord our God, king of the universe, Who
created joy and gladness, groom and bride, mirth, glad song,
pleasure, delight, love, brotherhood, peace, and companionship.
Lord, our God, let there soon be heard in the cities of Judah
and the streets of Jerusalem the sound of joy and the sound of
gladness, the voice of the groom and the voice of the bride, the
sound of the grooms' jubilance from their canopies and of youths
from their song-filled feasts. Blessed are You, who gladdens the
groom with the bride.

From "The Seven Blessings" of the marriage service

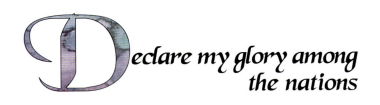

Declare my glory among the nations

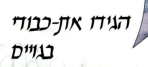

הגיד את־כבודי בגוים

ואנכי מעשיהם ומחשבתיהם באה לקבץ את־כל־הגוים והלשנות ובאו וראו
את־כבודי: ושמתי בהם אות ושלחתי מהם פליטים אל־הגוים תרשיש פול
ולוד משכי קשת תובל ויון האיים הרחקים אשר לא־שמעו את־שמעי ולא־ראו
את־כבודי והגידו את־כבודי בגוים: והביאו את־כל־אחיכם מכל־הגוים מנחה
ליהוה בסוסים וברכב ובצבים ובפרדים ובכרכרות על הר קדשי ירושלם אמר
יהוה כאשר יביאו בני ישראל את־המנחה בכלי טהור בית יהוה: וגם מהם
אקח לכהנים ללוים אמר יהוה.

ישעיה סו:יח-כא

For I know their works and their thoughts: the time shall
come, that I will gather all nations and tongues; and they shall
come, and see my glory. And I will set a sign among them, and
I will send those that escape of them of the nations, to Tarshish,
Pul, and Lud, that draw the bow, to Tuval, and Yavan, to the
distant islands, that have not heard my fame, and have not seen
my glory; and they shall declare my glory among the nations.
And they shall bring all your brethren out of all the nations for
an offering to the Lord upon horses, and in chariots, and in
litters, and upon mules, and upon fleet camels, to my holy
mountain Jerusalem, says the Lord, as the children of Israel
bring an offering in a clean vessel to the house of the Lord.
And I will also take of them for priests and for Levites, says
the Lord.

Isaiah 66:18-21

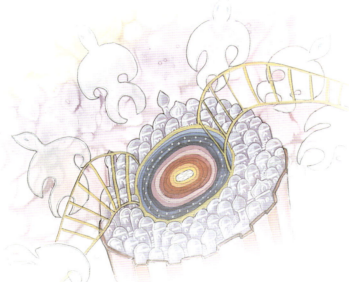

וכרתי להם ברית שלום ברית עולם יהיה אותם ונתתים והרביתי אותם ונתתי
את-מקדשי בתוכם לעולם: והיה משכני עליהם והייתי להם לאלהים והמה
יהיו-לי לעם: וידעו הגוים כי אני יהוה מקדש את-ישראל בהיות מקדשי
בתוכם לעולם.

יחזקאל לז:כו-כח

גדול יהיה כבוד הבית הזה האחרון מן-הראשון אמר יהוה צבאות ובמקום
הזה אתן שלום נאם יהוה צבאות.

חגי ב:ט

I will make a covenant of peace with them; it shall be an everlasting covenant with them, which I will give them; and I will multiply them, and will set my sanctuary in the midst of them for evermore. And my tabernacle shall be with them; and I will be their God, and they shall be my people. Then the nations shall know that I the Lord do sanctify Israel, when my sanctuary shall be in the midst of them for evermore.
Ezekiel 37:26-28

The glory of this latter house shall be greater than that of the former, says the Lord of Hosts; and in this place I will give peace, says the Lord of hosts.
Haggai 2:9

New heavens and a new earth

מים חדשים וארץ
חדשה

כי־הנני בורא שמים חדשים וארץ חדשה ולא תזכרנה הראשנות ולא תעלינה
על־לב: כי אם־שישו וגילו עדי־עד אשר אני בורא כי הנני בורא את־ירושלם
גילה ועמה פשוש: וגלתי בירושלם וששתי בעמי ולא־ישמע בה עוד קול
בכי וקול זעקה.

ישעיה סה:יז-יח

For, behold, I create new heavens and a new earth: and the
former things shall not be remembered, nor come to mind. But
be glad and rejoice for ever in that which I create: for, behold,
I create Jerusalem a rejoicing, and her people a joy. And I
will rejoice in Jerusalem, and joy in my people: and the voice
of weeping shall be not more heard in her, nor the voice of crying.

Isaiah 65:17-18

95-pl. 48

 **S**ong of praise

 שיר הלל

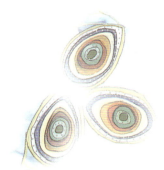

קול דודי הנה-זה בא מדלג על-ההרים מקפץ על-הגבעות: דומה דודי לצבי
או לעפר האילים הנה-זה עומד אחר כתלנו משגיח מן-החלנות מציץ מן-החרכים:
ענה דודי ואמר לי קומי לך רעיתי יפתי ולכי-לך: כי-הנה הסתו עבר הגשם
חלף הלך לו: הנצנים נראו בארץ עת הזמיר הגיע וקול התור נשמע בארצנו.
שיר השירים ב:ח-יב

The voice of my beloved! behold, he comes leaping upon the
mountains, skipping upon the hills. My beloved is like a gazelle
or a young hart: behold, he stands behind our wall, he looks in
at the windows; he peers through the lattice. My beloved spoke,
and said to me, Rise up, my love, my fair one, and come away.
For, lo, the winter is past, the rain is over and gone; the
flowers appear on the earth; the time of the singing bird is come,
and the voice of the turtle is heard in our land.
Song of Songs 2:8-12

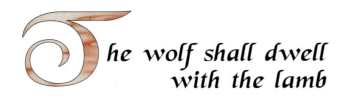

The wolf shall dwell with the lamb

גר זאב עם
כבש

וגר זאב עם-כבש ונמר עם-גדי ירבץ ועגל וכפיר ומריא יחדו ונער קטן נהג בם:
ופרה ודב תרעינה יחדו ירבצו ילדיהן ואריה כבקר יאכל-תבן: ושעשע יונק על-חר
פתן ועל מאורת צפעוני גמול ידו הדה: לא-ירעו ולא-ישחיתו בכל-הר קדשי
כי-מלאה הארץ דעה את-יהוה כמים לים מכסים.

ישעיה יא:ו-ט

The wolf also shall dwell with the lamb, and the leopard shall
lie down with the kid; and the calf and the young lion and the
fatling together; and a little child shall lead them. And the cow
and the bear shall feed; their young ones shall lie down together:
and the lion shall eat straw like the ox. And the sucking child
play on the hole of the cobra, and the weaned child shall put
his hand on the viper's nest. They shall not hurt nor destroy in
all my holy mountain: for the earth shall be full of the knowledge
of the Lord, as the waters cover the sea.

Isaiah 11:6-9

אני מאמין באמונה שלמה, בביאת המשיח ואף על פי שיתמהמה,

עם כל זה אחכה לו בכל יום שיבוא.

שלושה עשר עיקרים (רמב"ם)

I believe with total faith in the coming of the Messiah,
and even though he may delay, nevertheless I anticipate
every day that he will come.

The Thirteen Principles of Faith (Maimonides)

List of Plates